LOOKING INTO THE PAST:
PEOPLE, PLACES, AND CUSTOMS

National Flags

by

Dwayne E. Pickels

Chelsea House Publishers

CHELSEA HOUSE PUBLISHERS

Editor in Chief Stephen Reginald
Managing Editor James D. Gallagher
Production Manager Pamela Loos
Art Director Sara Davis
Picture Editor Judy Hasday
Senior Production Editor Lisa Chippendale
Designers Takeshi Takahashi, Keith Trego

First Printing.

1 3 5 7 9 8 6 4 2

Library of Congress Cataloging-in-Publication Data

Pickels, Dwayne E.
National flags / by Dwayne E. Pickels.

    p.   cm. — (Looking into the past)
Includes bibliographical references and index.
Summary: Describes the flags of twenty-five nations from
around the world and presents information about the location, population, history, current government, and capital
of each nation.

ISBN 0-7910-4686-9

1. Flags—Juvenile literature. [1.Flags.] I. Title. II. Series.
CR109.P53 1997   97-28951
929.9_2—dc21   CIP
                                                          AC

CONTENTS

CULTURE, CUSTOMS, AND RITUALS

The important moments of our lives—from birth through puberty, aging, and death—are made more meaningful by culture, customs, and rituals. But what is culture? The word *culture,* broadly defined, includes the way of life of an entire society. This encompasses customs, rituals, codes of manners, dress, languages, norms of behavior, and systems of beliefs. Individuals are both acted on by and react to a culture—and so generate new cultural forms and customs.

What is custom? Custom refers to accepted social practices that separate one cultural group from another. Every culture contains basic customs, often known as rites of transition or passage. These rites, or ceremonies, occur at different stages of life, from birth to death, and are sometimes religious in nature. In all cultures of the world today, a new baby is greeted and welcomed into its family through ceremony. Some ceremonies, such as the bar mitzvah, a religious initiation for teenage Jewish boys, mark the transition from childhood to adulthood. Marriage also is usually celebrated by a ritual of some sort. Death is another rite of transition. All known cultures contain beliefs about life after death, and all observe funeral rites and mourning customs.

What is a ritual? What is a rite? These terms are used interchangeably to describe a ceremony associated with a custom. The English ritual of shaking hands in greeting, for example, has become part of that culture. The washing of one's hands could be considered a ritual which helps a person achieve an accepted level of cleanliness—a requirement of the cultural beliefs that person holds.

The books in this series, *Looking into the Past: People,*

Places, and Customs, explore many of the most interesting rituals of different cultures through time. For example, did you know that in the year A.D. 1075 William the Conqueror ordered that a "Couvre feu" bell be rung at sunset in each town and city of England, as a signal to put out all fires? Because homes were made of wood and had thatched roofs, the bell served as a precaution against house fires. Today, this custom is no longer observed as it was 900 years ago, but the modern word *curfew* derives from its practice.

Another ritual that dates from centuries long past is the Japanese Samurai Festival. This colorful celebration commemorates the feats of the ancient samurai warriors who ruled the country hundreds of years ago. Japanese citizens dress in costumes, and direct descendants of warriors wear samurai swords during the festival. The making of these swords actually is a separate religious rite in itself.

Different cultures develop different customs. For example, people of different nations have developed various interesting ways to greet each other. In China 100 years ago, the ordinary salutation was a ceremonious, but not deep, bow, with the greeting "Kin t'ien ni hao ma?" (Are you well today?). During the same era, citizens of the Indian Ocean island nation Ceylon (now called Sri Lanka) greeted each other by placing their palms together with the fingers extended. When greeting a person of higher social rank, the hands were held in front of the forehead and the head was inclined.

Some symbols and rituals rooted in ancient beliefs are common to several cultures. For example, in China, Japan, and many of the countries of the East, a tortoise is a symbol of protection from black magic, while fish have represented fertility, new life, and prosperity since the beginnings of human civilization. Other ancient fertility symbols have been incorporated into religions we still practice today, and so these ancient beliefs remain a part of our civilization. A more recent belief, the legend of Santa Claus, is the story of a kind benefactor who brings gifts to the good children of the world. This story appears in the lore of nearly every nation. Each country developed its own variation on the legend and each celebrates Santa's arrival in a different way.

New rituals are being created all the time. On April 21, 1997, for example, the cremated remains of 24 people were launched into orbit around Earth on a Pegasus rocket. Included among the group whose ashes now head toward their "final frontier" are Gene Roddenberry, creator of the television series *Star Trek,* and Timothy Leary, a countercultural icon of the 1960s. Each person's remains were placed in a separate aluminum capsule engraved with the person's name and a commemorative phrase. The remains will orbit the Earth every 90 minutes for two to ten years. When the rocket does re-enter Earth's atmosphere, it will burn up with a great burst of light. This first-time ritual could become an accepted rite of passage, a custom in our culture that would supplant the current ceremonies marking the transition between life and death.

Curiosity about different customs, rites, and rituals dates back to the mercantile Greeks of classical times. Herodotus (484–425 B.C.), known as the "Father of History," described Egyptian culture. The Roman historian Tacitus (A.D. 55–117) similarly wrote a lengthy account about the customs of the "modern" European barbarians. From the Greeks to Marco Polo, from Columbus to the Pacific voyages of Captain James Cook, cultural differences have fascinated the literate world. The books in the *Looking into the Past* series collect the most interesting customs from many cultures of the past and explain their origins, meanings, and relationship to the present day.

In the future, space travel may very well provide the impetus for new cultures, customs, and rituals, which will in turn enthrall and interest the peoples of future millennia.

Fred L. Israel
The City College of the City University of New York

CONTRIBUTORS

Senior Consulting Editor FRED L. ISRAEL is an award-winning historian. He received the Scribe's Award from the American Bar Association for his work on the Chelsea House series *The Justices of the United States Supreme Court.* A specialist in early American history, he was general editor for Chelsea's *1897 Sears Roebuck Catalog.* Dr. Israel has also worked in association with Dr. Arthur M. Schlesinger, jr. on many projects, including *The History of U.S. Presidential Elections* and *The History of U.S. Political Parties.* They are currently working together on the Chelsea House series *The World 100 Years Ago*, which looks at the traditions, customs, and cultures of many nations at the turn of the century.

DWAYNE E. PICKELS is an award-winning reporter with the *Greensburg (Pa.) Tribune-Review.* A Magna Cum Laude graduate of the University of Pittsburgh, where he cofounded the literary magazine *Pendulum,* Dwayne won a Pennsylvania Newspaper Publishers' Association (PNPA) Keystone Press Award in 1992. He currently resides in Scottdale, Pa., with his wife, Mary, and their daughter, Kaidia Leigh. In his free time, he is currently immersed in a number of literary pursuits—which include a novel based on Celtic myth and legend. In addition to writing, Dwayne enjoys outdoor excursions, including bird watching, hiking, photography, and target shooting…along with typically futile attempts at fishing.

OVERVIEW
Symbols of the Great Nations

E ach nation that makes up the vastly varied hodge-podge we call the world community boasts a proud and fascinating history filled with tales of triumph and tragedy. Some countries have existed for centuries, while others have emerged only within our lifetimes—yet each is valid and worthy of understanding in its uniqueness.

It is precisely the diversity of the world's nations that makes one symbol above all others important to each political unit that marks off boundaries on the globe, and that is its flag. The flag of a nation—a patterned image made of fabric, color, and design—is its identity, its voice in the din of the international chorus.

Some flags indicate a nation's past, such as the flag of the United States, with its stars representing the 50 states and its stripes representing the 13 original American colonies. Other nations reflect religious or political symbols in the design of their flags, such as Turkey, which includes symbols of Islam, the country's major religion.

Filled with symbolism and national pride, a country's flag is the one symbol that most clearly speaks to its own people and to neighbors near and far of all tongues. Some flags represent a sense of freedom; others show loyal allegiance to a homeland. But whether they reflect a glorious past or a hope for a fruitful future, flags have been and will remain symbols of glory and honor throughout the world.

Not all of the illustrations in this book depict a nation's

current national flag, however; some show flags from various periods in a nation's history. In this book, we will examine the past or present flags of 25 nations from around the world—learning a little about each of the various countries, and people, for which these proud rectangular symbols stand. Specifically, we will investigate each nation's location, population, history, current government, and capital as we look into the meanings woven into its flag's design.

ALBANIA

Situated along the shores of the Adriatic Sea in southern Europe, the People's Socialist Republic of Albania is one of the smaller countries of the Balkan Peninsula. With some 11,000 square miles of mountainous land in a Mediterranean climate, Albania abuts the nations of Greece, Montenegro, Macedonia, Kosovo, and Yugoslavia, and sits just across the Strait of Otranto from the "heel" of Italy's "boot."

Albania's original national flag, pictured at left, was distinguished by a brilliant field marked by a black double-headed eagle positioned beneath a red star outlined in yellow. Said to have been taken from the state coat of arms, the eagle was originally the symbol of the Byzantine Empire—which dominated the country during its early history, following years of rule by neighboring Greeks and Romans. These periods were followed by invasions by Goths, Slavs, and Normans prior to Albania being conquered by Islamic Turks during the 1400s.

The nation's independence was finally won in 1912, during the first Balkan War. Albania was later proclaimed a socialist republic in 1946—the same year the present format of its flag was adopted. Sources indicate the red background of the country's flag was chosen to symbolize blood Albanians shed in struggles against the Turks and the other invading forces, while the five-pointed star is said to represent the fundamentals of communism.

Though Albania is officially cited as an atheist nation, its population of roughly 3,197,000 is primarily of Muslim faith, with Roman Catholic and Greek Orthodox minorities. Albania's capital is Tiranë.

POLAND

POLAND

Poland's national flag consists of two large horizontal stripes, white over red, each taking up half of the flag. The colors, reportedly culled from the state coat of arms, are said to have been selected in 1831. However, they were not actually incorporated into the flag until 1919.

Various interpretations exist regarding the meaning of the flag's simple design. One is that the flag symbolizes a white eagle soaring over a setting sun, while another is that the design represents the idea of trading human blood for freedom. A more modern proposal simply cites the nation's hope to live peacefully in socialism.

Historians say that Slavic tribes first united to form the Polish state around the 10th century. Subsequent eras saw a number of forces invade Poland, including Russians in the 17th century. By the early 1900s, Poland was established as an independent country—though it was a short-lived freedom. Nazi Germany invaded in 1939, decimating much of the country. When the Axis forces were defeated by Allied forces in 1945, a provisional government established under Soviet auspices left communists in control, and Poland was declared a socialist republic in 1952.

Within the past decade, Poland emerged from domination by the Soviet Union. In 1989, a ban on Solidarity (an independent trade union organization) was lifted and the first free elections were held, with Solidarity Party leader Lech Walesa winning the presidency in 1990. Most of Poland's 37.9 million people are of the Roman Catholic faith. Its capital is Warsaw.

SPAIN

Spain

With some 195,000 square miles of land, including the Balearic and Canary Islands, Spain comprises the largest portion of the Iberian Peninsula of southwestern Europe, which it shares with Portugal. Spain lies south of the Pyrenees Mountains from its other neighbor, France.

Said to have been derived from the medieval coat of arms of its Aragon region, the Spanish flag is distinguished by a large yellow horizontal bar flanked by two smaller horizontal red bars, one above and one below. The current incarnation of this flag, adopted in 1981, is slightly different from the flag pictured in the illustration, which boasts an eagle in the yellow field. Amid its red-yellow-red field is a coat of arms—a quartered shield bearing images of a castle, a lion wearing a crown of gold, red stripes, and red chains—topped with a larger crown and situated between two ornate columns wrapped in a banner that reads *plus ultra*, a Latin phrase that means "there is more beyond."

Settled in ancient times by Celts, Phoenicians, and Greeks, Spain was conquered by Rome in the second century. Following invasions by Vandals and Moors, Christian forces gradually retook the territory.

Spain was established as an independent nation in 1492 under the rule of King Ferdinand V of Aragon and Queen Isabella of Castile—the same monarchs who financed the famous voyages of Christopher Columbus. Today Spain is a constitutional monarchy with a population of 39.2 million. Its capital is Madrid and its primary religion is Roman Catholicism.

Tourism is the country's number one industry.

ENGLAND

Settled by ancient Celts, and later conquered by Romans, Angles, Saxons, Normans, and others, England rose to become the center one of the world's grandest empires. That's no small feat for a country that's essentially an island in the northern Atlantic Ocean. Though it lays claim to some 94,000 square miles of land mass, England—also known as Great Britain—is entirely surrounded by water. England is the largest of the nations that make up what is geographically known as the British Isles, along with Ireland, Scotland, and Wales. Politically, these islands compose the United Kingdom of England and Northern Ireland.

The flag pictured at left is the English flag. Another well-known flag of the United Kingdom is called the "Union Jack" by many around the world. With a blue field traversed by thick red and white crossed bands over a similar but thinner "X" pattern, this flag is a conglomerate of several earlier designs attributed to patron saints of England, Ireland, and Scotland. It was created in 1801 as a result of the legislative union between the nations.

Today, the United Kingdom has a population of a little more than 57 million. With its capital in London, the nation is governed under a constitutional monarchy system, in which the monarch plays a purely symbolic role. Actual duties of government are conducted by a prime minister and Parliament, a representative legislature. There are two divisions of England's Parliament—the House of Lords, members of which hold seats as a privilege of rank, and the House of Commons, members of which are elected.

FRANCE

FRANCE

France, a republic in western Europe, is bordered to the south by Spain. Italy, Switzerland, Germany, and Belgium are its neighbors to the east, while to the north, Great Britain lies just across the English Channel.

At roughly 200,000 square miles in size, France is home to nearly 56 million people, making it the third-largest country in Europe. France is well known as a world leader in making high-quality wines and cognac—a brandy-like spirit named after the country's Cognac region, where grapes used in its production are grown.

With its vertical red, white, and blue stripes, the French flag was first presented in its current configuration in 1794, in the wake of the French Revolution. It is said to have been based upon another tricolored flag—that of the Netherlands, which has the same color scheme in a horizontal pattern.

Originally settled by Gauls and Romans, over the centuries France has been one of the great world powers, conquering and occupying territories around the globe under famous leaders such as Charlemagne and Napoleon. At one time, the French even held large overseas territories on the continent of North America, primarily in Canada. However, France itself was occupied by Nazi Germany during World War II.

With its capital in Paris, France today is governed by a president, elected every seven years, as well as a prime minister and two legislative houses—the Senate and National Assembly.

TURKEY

ith coastline on the Black, Aegean, and Mediterranean seas, the Republic of Turkey is situated primarily in Asia Minor, with a small portion of territory across the Bosporus in southeastern Europe.

Turkey's neighbors include Greece and Bulgaria to the west, Iraq and Syria to the south, Iran and Armenia to the east, and Georgia to the north. Turkey contains some 301,000 square miles of territory, and is home to roughly 55.6 million people. Its capital is Ankara.

The Turkish flag is a bold red field with a simple white crescent moon design and a white five-pointed star—long-time symbols of Islam—situated slightly left of center. This present pattern dates to 1844, though for a three-year period in the 1920s, the flag had a green background. The flag is also said to have been a model for the flag of Tunisia, which bears a more abstract crescent and star pattern in red, placed within a white circle on a red field.

While the Turks themselves are largely descended from Tartars who migrated into Asia Minor in the 11th century, various civilizations have been centered in the region from as far back as 7000 B.C. Through the ages, Turkey has been part of nearly a half-dozen empires, including the powerful Ottoman Empire that conquered and ruled large portions of that region of the world for many years.

Declared a republic in 1923, Turkey today is governed by a president, elected every seven years, as well as a prime minister and one legislative house, the Grand National Assembly. The primary religion of the nation is Islam, though a small Christian minority exists.

JAPAN

hough it has only about 146,000 square miles of land area, the tiny island nation of Japan is home to more than 123 million people, making it one of the most densely populated nations in the world.

Known as the Land of the Rising Sun, Japan is located off the eastern coast of Asia. It is made up of four major mountainous islands, as well as some 500 smaller isles and about 3,000 minor islands.

With a simple stark white field serving as backdrop to a bright red circle in the center, Japan's flag is called *Hi-no-maru*, or "the sun disc." Originally held by the nation's shogun dictators, the banner became the official national flag in 1870. To the Japanese, the white field symbolizes purity, while the red "sun" is said to represent passion.

The highly recognizable flag in the illustration, with its rays shooting from the sun disk, marked the sides of the fighter planes and bombers that propelled Japan into World War II with a surprise attack on the United States' Pacific naval fleet in Pearl Harbor, Hawaii, on December 7, 1941—sinking 19 ships and causing more than 2,000 casualties. However, in 1945, Japan surrendered in the wake of two devastating nuclear bombings at Hiroshima and Nagasaki, which resulted in the utter destruction of both cities and the deaths of more than 150,000 people.

Proving itself a resilient nation, Japan has since seen a resurgence in economic, social, and cultural vitality, largely due to highly competitive industrial and technological advances. The Japanese government is a constitutional monarchy with an emperor, as well as a prime minister and two legislative bodies—the House of Councilors and House of Representatives. Its capital is Tokyo.

TIBET

Perched atop a lofty plateau in central Asia—and home to the highest mountain chain in the world—Tibet has earned the nickname the Roof of the World.

Tibet is bordered by the countries of Burma, India, Nepal, Bhutan, and Sikkim. With an average elevation of 15,000 feet above sea level, the country encompasses some 472,000 square miles of territory, which includes the towering Himalayan Mountains.

This high heritage seems to be evident in the nation's flag, which bears a large golden sun casting streaming rays of red and blue. But within the lower region of the flag, beneath the sun symbol, two lion images face each other atop a white triangular shape—assumed to represent a snow-covered peak. The icon is likely representative of Mount Everest, the world's tallest peak, which soars some 29,028 feet above sea level. An ornate border pattern also adorns the flag's horizontal edges, as well as its "hoist"—the vertical edge nearest the flagpole. This design, however, does not grace the remaining vertical edge.

Once a powerful kingdom in its own right, Tibet fell under Chinese rule in the early 1700s. The Chinese were successfully driven out in 1911 but reinvaded the country in 1950. Following a brutally suppressed revolution in 1959, and annexation by China in 1965, Tibet remains occupied by Chinese forces, though unrest continues.

Led by the Dalai Lama and the Panchen Lama, Tibetans traditionally practiced Buddhist Lamaism as their primary religion. Tibet's capital is Lhasa.

ITALY

Even the most geographically challenged map enthusiasts have little trouble locating the Republic of Italy, thanks to the distinctive "boot" shape of this peninsula that extends into the Mediterranean Sea from southern Europe. Perhaps as recognizable is the nation's flag—though that may not always have been the case.

Similar in design to the flags of France and Ireland, the tricolored Italian flag of equal thirds green, white, and red (from left, or hoist, to right) once bore the royal coat of arms of the House of Savoy. The silver cross on a red shield was added on orders of Victor Emmanuel II, king of Sardinia-Piedmont, in the 1800s. The symbol was removed when Italy was declared a republic in 1946.

Though Italy today contains only some 116,000 square miles of territory, including the islands of Sicily and Sardinia, it was once the center of one of the largest empires of the ancient world. Early in its history, Rome was sacked by marauding Celts, who later abandoned the city. A few centuries later, under the leadership of Julius Caesar, Roman legions returned the favor, driving Celts out of Gaul (France) and the rest of mainland Europe and into the British Isles, which Roman forces also occupied for some time during the first century A.D. Rome also conquered many other regions and civilizations before the empire's ultimate collapse before 500 A.D.

Today the nation of roughly 57 million people is governed by a president, a prime minister, and two legislative bodies—the Senate and Chamber of Deputies. Rome also remains home to Vatican City, a separate state and the headquarters of the Roman Catholic Church.

ICELAND

ICELAND

onsidered the second largest island of Europe, the Republic of Iceland is situated in the northern Atlantic Ocean, northwest of Scotland's Faroe Islands and only some 650 miles southeast of Greenland.

Viking explorers are said to have discovered Iceland late in the first century A.D., and it remained under Norwegian rule until the latter portion of the 1200s. Danish rule of Iceland reportedly ensued around 1380.

Officially adopted in 1915, Iceland's flag is a dark blue field with two red-on-white bars crossing in the hoist-side third, in a pattern said to symbolize a Scandinavian cross. The flag is similar to Norway's, with its colors reversed.

Today, Iceland is home to some 252,000 hearty inhabitants of Scandinavian stock who share the beautiful but rugged and unforgiving terrain of nearly 40,000 square miles. Situated just south of the Arctic Circle, Iceland features summer temperatures that average in the low 50° F range. The island is home to more than 100 volcanoes in various stages of activity, creating a number of hot springs, geysers, and lava fields. There are also a number of mammoth glaciers with which inhabitants contend.

Considering these environmental conditions, it's not too difficult to fathom why the colors of Iceland's flag are said to represent the sea (blue), volcanic lava (red), and icy glaciers (white).

Though it has been self-governing since 1918, Iceland was declared a republic in 1944. Its capital is Reykjavik, and the most prominent religion among its people today is Evangelical Lutheran.

AMERICA

U.S.A.

ome to well over 250 million people from virtually all ethnic origins, the United States of America is commonly known as "the melting pot." Flanked by Mexico to the south and Canada to the north, the U.S. spans the entire mid-region of the North American continent, from the Atlantic Ocean in the east to the Pacific Ocean in the west. Alaska, located on the far northwestern rim of Canada, and the Hawaiian Islands in the Pacific, are also counted among its 50 states.

Though dispute remains over who actually discovered the "New World," it was already home to numerous tribes of Native Americans when early European settlers began to arrive around the 16th century. By the 1700s, England controlled most of the colonized territories along America's eastern seaboard. However, those colonies formed an independent union in 1776, which was cemented in military victory over England in 1783. A major westward expansion followed this Revolutionary War, opening the door to an immense wave of immigration such as no other country in the world has ever seen.

Perhaps the most recognized symbol in the entire world, the current U.S. flag includes 13 horizontal stripes (seven red and six white) with a blue corner field containing 50 five-pointed white stars arranged in nine alternating rows of six and five. Its stripes represent the 13 colonies that formed the original Union, while the stars represent the current number of states. The present format, dating to 1960, is the 27th version of the U.S. flag.

From its capital in Washington, D.C., the U.S.A. is governed by a president, elected every four years, and two representative legislative bodies, the Senate and the House of Representatives.

CHINA

With nearly 3.7 million square miles of land and 1.1 billion people, the People's Republic of China is the world's third largest nation in area, and the largest in population.

China is also considered one of the world's oldest civilizations. Its culture, which dates back some 3,500 years into the past, has produced a number of well-known ruling dynasties that have yielded great thinkers, such as Confucius, and many inventions and innovations.

A civil war between the Chinese Communist Party and the Nationalist Party began in 1927, but it was suspended temporarily to thwart the Japanese invasion during World War II in the 1940s. However, the conflict erupted once again in 1945, ending with the Communists' victory in 1949.

The flag pictured at left is the flag of the Chinese Republic, which was overthrown by the Communists. China's current red-fielded flag is said to have been inspired by the flag of its largest neighbor, the former Soviet Union. Other abutting countries include Afghanistan, Mongolia, North Korea, Vietnam, Laos, Burma, Nepal, and India. While it originally bore a striking similarity to the Russian flag, the Chinese replaced the hammer and sickle logo with a large solid yellow five-pointed star flanked on the right by four smaller stars in the upper hoist-side corner. Adopted in 1949, the large star is said to represent the Communist Party and the four smaller stars are supposed to symbolize workers, peasants, bourgeoisie, and capitalists.

With its capital in Beijing, formerly known as Peking, the People's Republic of China is now governed by a president, a premier, and a legislative house, the National People's Congress.

MEXICO

MEXICO

roperly known as the United Mexican States, Mexico is a officially Spanish-speaking nation—though only about 10 percent of its people are actually believed to be of purely Spanish descent.

Bordered on the north by the United States and on the south by the Central American countries of Guatemala and Belize, Mexico is flanked by the Caribbean Sea and the Gulf of Mexico to the east and the Pacific Ocean to the west. Some 88.3 million people inhabit Mexico's 756,000 square miles of total geography, located in the far southern reaches of the continent of North America.

Mexico's flag is a tricolored design bearing three vertical stripes in green, white, and red. In the center of the flag is a state coat of arms that shows a brown eagle perched atop a cactus and clenching a green serpent in its beak. The ornate design is said to be illustrative of an old Aztec legend. And though the flag has undergone several design alterations since it was first introduced in 1821, its present format has not changed since 1968.

Archaelogical evidence indicates that Mexico may have been inhabited by native peoples as far back as 10,000 B.C. The Aztecs—the last great pre-Columbian civilization in Mexico—were conquered by Spanish invaders in the 1500s. These "explorers" founded a colony in Mexico called New Spain, and Spanish rule continued until Mexico's independence was proclaimed in 1821. Today, Mexico is a federal republic governed by presidents elected every six years and two legislative houses, the Senate and the Chamber of Deputies. Its capital is located in Mexico City.

IRELAND

The Republic of Ireland (known in Gaelic as Eire) is located in the western region of the British Isles in the northern Atlantic Ocean. Roughly one-sixth of the island nation is occupied by a separate political entity, Northern Ireland.

With only 27,000 square miles of land, the Republic of Ireland has 3.5 million inhabitants, who speak primarily English and Gaelic, the language of the pagan Celtic civilization that evolved there around 400 B.C. Following the introduction of Christianity and subsequent epochs marked by invasions of Vikings and Anglo-Normans, Ireland formed a union with England in 1801. An armed resistance in the wake of World War I resulted in some measure of independence from Great Britain in 1921. The cause was then taken up through terroristic measures by Irish Republican Army (IRA) soldiers, who are still active today in Northern Ireland, though the remainder of the country left the British Commonwealth and formed an independent republic in 1949.

A version of Ireland's present flag—a basic tricolored design of green, white and orange—replaced a previous emerald field with a yellow harp around the 1830s. The current design, adopted in 1920, was officially confirmed in the Constitution of 1937. The three colors are symbolic: green represents the Emerald Isle and the Catholic majority; orange, the Protestants; and white, the need for peace and unity between the two feuding groups.

With its capital located in Dublin, Ireland is governed by a president, elected every seven years, as well as a prime minister and two legislative houses, the Senate and the House of Deputies.

AUSTRIA

The central European nation Austria is well known for producing some of the most talented musicians and composers the world has ever seen, including Wolfgang Amadeus Mozart, Franz Joseph Haydn, and Franz Schubert, among many others.

Though it is bordered by Switzerland, Italy, Liechtenstein, Hungary, the Czech Republic, Slovenia, Slovakia, and Germany, 98 percent of Austria's 7.6 million people are of German descent. German is also the nation's official language. Settled first by peoples of Celtic origin, the area later fell under Roman dominion and subsequently was invaded by a number of tribes, including Vandals, Goths, and Huns.

Austria's original flag, consisting of a red-white-red horizontal bar field, is one of the oldest in the world. On Austria's current flag, this pattern was reproduced on a shield on the chest of a gold-crowned black eagle centered on the flag. In the eagle's talons are a gold hammer and a sickle. The present format was adopted in 1918, the same year Austria became an independent republic under the Treaty of Versailles. Though it was occupied once again by Nazi German forces beginning in 1938, independence returned with the Allied victory in 1945. This event also affected the country's flag, as, after the fall of the Third Reich, an image of broken silver chains has appeared on the eagle's legs as a symbol of Austria's liberation.

Today, with 33,000 square miles of land, the Federal Republic of Austria is governed by a president, elected every six years, and a chancellor, who is appointed by the president. Its two legislative bodies are called Federal and National councils, and Austria's capital is Vienna.

THAILAND

THALAND

Once called the Land of the White Elephant, Thailand is a constitutional monarchy located in southeastern Asia. Formerly known as Siam, Thailand is situated on the northern shores of the Gulf of Siam and is bordered by Myanmar, Laos, Cambodia, and Malaysia.

Thailand's people are primarily descended from Mongols who probably migrated from southern China around 1,000 B.C. Nearly 3,000 years later, in 1939, Thailand was proclaimed an independent monarchy. Not long afterward, however, the country was invaded and occupied by Japan during World War II. A series of military coups have since kept the nation of roughly 198,000 square miles and more than 55 million people in a state of political turmoil that has endured into the 1990s.

Thailand's flag is centered by a horizontal blue band shrouded by two horizontal white bars and then two red stripes, also running horizontally. The colors are said to represent royalty (blue), Buddhism and national purity (white), and the blood shed to earn freedom (red). Though the flag once bore a white elephant, that symbol was omitted in 1917, and the flag's present form has not changed since then.

Thai, otherwise known as Siamese, is the country's official language, and Hinayana Buddhism is its official religion. Despite its small geographical size, Thailand is one of the world's leading exporters of rice. From its capital in Bangkok, this country is governed by a king and a prime minister. However, in a format that resembles that of the United States, a Senate and House of Representatives make up Thailand's legislature, the National Assembly.

INDIA

INDIA

A federal union of 22 states and nine territories located in south central Asia, the Republic of India is the largest nation on Asia's Indian subcontinent—a region it shares with the neighboring countries of Pakistan, Bangladesh, Nepal, and Myanmar.

To the north of India stands the vast, high Himalayan Mountains, while on its western shores lies the Arabian Sea. The Bay of Bengal is located to the east, and the Indian Ocean is directly south, beyond the tiny island nation of Sri Lanka. India also borders China, the only country in the world with a greater population. At 1.3 million square miles in size, India is home to nearly 836 million people—most of whom still live in small villages and observe the Hindu faith.

The Indian flag bears three horizontal stripes in orange, white, and green. Centered in the middle (white) stripe is a blue rendering of Emperor Asoka's *dharma chakra*, or "wheel of life"—a sunlike symbol of Indian culture that is also incorporated into India's state coat of arms. It contains 24 rays to mark the hours in the day, while its color, blue, symbolizes sea and sky. The flag was adopted in 1947, following declaration of India's independence from British rule.

From its capital in New Delhi, India today is governed by a president, elected every five years, and a prime minister, as well as two legislative bodies, the Council of States and the House of the People.

SWEDEN

estled between Norway and Finland in the Scandinavian peninsula of northern Europe, Sweden shares the shores of the Baltic Sea with Lithuania, Latvia, Estonia, and Poland to the southeast. Denmark lies not far offshore to the southwest.

Sweden's 8.5 million people share a little over 170,000 square miles of terrain with a varied climate. In its southern realms, winters are brief and mild, while in its frigid north, Sweden's winter seasons are long and harsh.

The flag of Sweden bears a powder-blue field unequally divided by a yellow Scandinavian cross. Some sources indicate it may have been inspired by the strikingly similar Danish flag—which is red with a white cross, and is said to be the oldest of the Nordic countries to use the symbol in a flag. Nonetheless, the design and color scheme of Sweden's flag may also be traced to the country's coat of arms, marked by gold crossed bars that divide four blue sections of shield. And though the origins of its flag may date back as far as the 1500s, its present form was not officially adopted until 1906—nearly a century after Sweden's government became a constitutional monarchy in 1809.

Sweden's government today is headed by a monarch and a prime minister. Stockholm is the capital, and most Swedes accept the Lutheran tenets of the Christian faith.

GREECE

GREECE

ong known as a bastion of civilized social order, Greece today contains over 10 million people in its approximately 51,000 square mile territory in southeastern Europe.

Greece is situated at the base of the Balkan Peninsula, and a fair portion of its geographical area comes from a multitude of islands, the largest being Crete. It is surrounded by the Ionian, Aegean, and Mediterranean Seas to the west, east and south. To the north are the countries of Albania, Macedonia, Bulgaria, and Turkey.

The flag of Greece bears a total of nine horizontal bars—four white and five blue. A white cross is centered on a top left (hoist-side) corner field of the same color blue, shades of which have varied over the years. Officially adopted as the nation's flag in 1822, it is said to represent "God's wisdom, freedom, and the country."

Historians consider ancient Greece to have been one of the major "cradles" of civilization, and the Greeks of antiquity are known for their stunning cultural advances and achievements. But, although the Greek conquerer Alexander the Great held a vast empire until his death in 323 B.C., modern times have not been as kind. Greece was conquered by Turkish forces in the 15th century and became part of the Ottoman Empire. Some 300 years later—following an eight-year war for independence—an independent constitutional monarchy was established in 1830.

Greece again suffered three years of occupation by Nazi German forces during World War II, which was immediately followed by a five-year civil war. A constitutional republic was established in 1975, with a president, prime minister, and one legislative body overseeing government in the nation's capital, Athens.

NEW ZEALAND

NEW ZEALAND

A sovereign state within the Commonwealth of Nations, the island nation of New Zealand is located more than 1,000 miles off the southeastern coast of Australia.

There, in the southwestern reaches of the Pacific Ocean, its two main islands, called "North Island" and "South Island," as well as its numerous minor islands, offer nearly 104,000 square miles of land to its 3.4 million inhabitants—most of whom are descendants of British settlers from the 1800s.

The flag of New Zealand incorporates the blue British "Ensign"—which is another name for a flag that is typically used on seagoing vessels. Also known as the "Union Jack," the well-known design appears in New Zealand's flag in the top hoist-side (left) corner of a dark blue field.

The remainder of the flag is filled with four five-pointed red stars trimmed in white. While these stars initially seem to be arranged in circular or random pattern, they actually represent the Southern Cross constellation, which is visible in skies below the Earth's equator. New Zealand's flag was first introduced for use on government ships in 1869, and it was later officially adopted as the national flag in 1902.

Granted a constitution for self-government in 1853, New Zealand was proclaimed a constitutional monarchy under treaty in 1947. Governmental duties in New Zealand today are handled by a governor, who represents the British Crown, as well as a local prime minister and a House of Representatives.

The nation's capital is Wellington.

NETHERLANDS

NETHERLANDS

Though their home is incorrectly but popularly known as Holland, the 15 million or so Dutch people so well known for wooden shoes, canals and dikes, and windmills are actually residents of the Netherlands. A small country of about 16,000 square miles situated across the North Sea from England to the west, Netherlands is bordered to the east by Germany and to the south by Belgium.

The Dutch flag consists of three horizontal stripes in red, white, and blue. It is said to have originated from the flag of Prince William of Orange, who led a revolt of Dutch Protestant provinces against Spanish rule in the late 1500s. The French flag—which uses the same color scheme in a vertical pattern—was reportedly based on the Netherlands' flag, and is said to have inspired the flag of Luxembourg, which is identical to the Dutch flag in all but its shade of blue. The flag of the Netherlands, which was officially adopted with a cobalt blue in 1937, is much darker.

Two stereotypical features of the Netherlands—windmills and dikes—stem from the nation's practice of reclaiming land from the sea by building dikes, or dams, to contain an area's water, and then pumping out the water to create fertile farmland. Previously, windmills were used to harness power for the pumps, though electricity is more widely used today.

Amsterdam is the capital of the Netherlands, but the Hague is the seat of Netherlands' constitutional monarchy, which was established in 1814. Today, the country's government is a parliamentary democracy. Netherlands Antilles, two groups of Caribbean islands also called the West Indies, remain Dutch territories.

RUSSIA

RUSSIA

Despite the breakup of the Soviet Union, or the Union of Soviet Socialist Republics (U.S.S.R.), Russia remains the largest country in the world in total area.

With a staggering 8.6 million square miles of land, Russia spans the entire northern region of the continent of Asia and more than half of Europe. Its 287 million inhabitants belong to more than 100 individual ethnic backgrounds.

The flag of the U.S.S.R., pictured at left, was a basic red field with a yellow hammer and sickle crossed beneath the small yellow outline of a five-pointed star near the top hoist-side corner. The symbols, taken from the state coat of arms, represented the union of workers and peasants under the leadership of the Communist Party. The red field represented the proletarian revolution.

Initially approved in a nearly identical format in 1924, the flag was slightly altered to its final version in 1955—though it was mandated in 1980 that the hammer-sickle-star pattern would appear only on one side of the flag.

Under the leadership of Lenin and the Bolshevik Party, the Soviet Union was established in the capital city of Moscow in 1922. Following an uneasy alliance with the United States against Nazi Germany during World War II, relations with the U.S. and other Western democracies entered a state of "cold war" —which ended in recent years when the Soviet government collapsed under economic strain on Dec. 25, 1991, the date upon which the independence of the 12 former Soviet republics was recognized.

SAUDI-ARABIA

SAUDI ARABIA

Perhaps best known for its vast oil fields, Saudi Arabia occupies a majority of the Arabian Peninsula of southwestern Asia. Primarily a desert nation, it is home to some 13.6 million mostly Islamic inhabitants who share approximately 865,000 square miles of largely inhospitable terrain. Saudi Arabia's hot, arid interior deserts, where temperatures can reach more than 120° F, are void of lakes and rivers, and some areas go without rainfall for years at a time.

Saudi Arabia is bordered by Jordan, Kuwait, and Iraq to the north, Yemen to the south, and Oman, the United Arab Emirates, and Qatar to the east. Iran lies across the Persian Gulf to the east, while across the Red Sea to the west are Egypt and Sudan.

The flag of Saudi Arabia is a brilliant green with a white Arabic inscription emblazoned in the center above a white scimitar-shaped sword design. The green field is said to represent the color of Islam and Muhammad, while the sword symbolizes military prowess. The words translate as a Muslim creed: "There is no God but Allah, and Muhammad is his prophet." In this incarnation, the flag was adopted in 1973.

Saudi Arabia fell under rule of the Turkish Ottoman Empire in the 1500s, though most of the region was eventually retaken in the 1700s, and the modern monarch-ruled nation was founded in the early 1900s. The nation's capital is Riyadh.

Saudi Arabia joined the alliance against Iraq during the Persian Gulf War in 1991. It still plays a major role in the Organization of Petroleum Exporting Countries (OPEC).

CANADA

CANADA

Spanning six time zones, Canada's staggering 3.8 million square miles of territory make it the second-largest country in the world, though it is also one of the world's least densely populated countries.

Occupying the northern third of the continent of North America, Canada is bordered to the south by the United States and stretches north beyond the Arctic Circle, nearly to the North Pole. However, with roughly two-thirds of its present population of some 26 million inhabiting urban centers near its southern borders, the country's vast northern regions remain primarily pristine wilderness.

The field of the easily recognizable Canadian flag is composed of a vertical white bar between two similar vertical red bars. But the flag's identifying characteristic is found in the center of the white bar—a red maple leaf design, which has been the country's national symbol for well over 100 years. The flag, in its present form, was introduced in 1965. The flag shown here is an earlier one, which illustrates Canada's link with the United Kingdom by its inclusion of the Union Jack in the hoist-side corner of the red field.

Settled by French explorers, Canada became a royal colony called New France in the 1600s. However, by 1763, the territory had proclaimed its allegiance to Great Britain. In 1867, Canada was established as a autonomous dominion under the British North American Act and formally remains a constitutional monarchy under the British Crown, though separatist tensions have persisted in French-speaking regions.

ECUADOR

ECUADOR

The Republic of Ecuador in South America takes its name from the Spanish word for equator, the imaginary line that separates the Earth into northern and southern hemispheres. The nation's capital, Quito, is situated almost precisely on this dividing line.

Ecuador's flag bears horizontal stripes of yellow, blue, and red, in a pattern very similar to neighboring Colombia's flag. However, it includes in the center the country's distinct coat of arms—an Andean condor perched atop an oval-shaped shield that is emblazoned with a landscape scene containing a variety of meaningful symbols. Though it had been in use since 1860, the flag was officially adopted in 1900.

Located on the northwestern coast of the continent of South America, Ecuador is bordered by Colombia to the north and Peru to the east and south. To its western side is the Pacific Ocean, where Ecuador's territory includes the exotic Galápagos Islands, some 650 miles offshore. With roughly 105,000 square miles of mostly mountainous terrain, Ecuador is home to some 10.5 million people. Two chains of the Andes mountain range locate some of the highest peaks in South America within the country.

Ecuador was liberated from Spanish rule in 1822 and was proclaimed an independent republic in 1830. Today, Ecuador is governed by a president and one legislative house, the National Congress. Its economic base largely shifted from agriculture to the petroleum industry in the early 1970s.

A Timeline of World Flags:

Dates of Official Adoption of Present Flag Formats

1794 – France

1801 – England

1844 – Turkey

1870 – Japan

1900 – Ecuador

1902 – New Zealand

1906 – Sweden

1915 – Iceland

1917 – Thailand

1918 – Austria

1919 – Poland

1922 – Ireland

1937 – Netherlands

1946 – Albania

1946 – Italy

1947 – India

1949 – China

1955 – Russia (former U.S.S.R.)

1960 – U.S.A.

1965 – Canada

1965 – Tibet

1968 – Mexico

1973 – Saudi Arabia

1978 – Greece

1981 – Spain

INDEX

FURTHER READING

Campbell, Gordon. *The Book of Flags*. London: Oxford University Press, 1953.

Contini, Mila. *Fashion: From Ancient Egypt to the Present Day*. New York: Cressent Books, 1965.

Crampton, William G. *Webster's Concise Encyclopedia of Flags & Coats of Arms*. New York: Cressent Books, 1985.

Harkavy, Michael D. (editor-in-chief). *The New Webster's International Encyclopedia*. Naples, Florida: Trident Press International, 1994.

Lister, Margot. *Costume: An Illustrated Survey from Ancient Times to the 20th Century*. Boston: Play's Inc, 1968.

Wilcox, R. Turner. *Folk and Festival Costume of the World*. New York: Charles Scribner's Sons, 1965.

MAY 3 1998